E

The Great War Diary of a Tadcaster Man

Mark and Jeremy Swinden

ISBN No: 978-1-904446-70-5

The proceeds from the sale of this book will go to good causes.

Published and printed by
Quacks Books
7 Grape Lane
Petergate
York YO1 7HU

Preface

The "Great War Diary of Edward E. Iredale" records his initial posting to France and covers the period 15th April 1915 to 7th December 1915 at which point, having been wounded, he was repatriated to the United Kingdom to recuperate. Having done so, he was posted to France again where he was killed in action, on the Somme, having been hit by shrapnel. He lost his life on 29th August 1916.

The diary Edward wrote was written in pencil and has not survived. Fortunately for posterity, his niece, Betty Iredale, the daughter of William Wilkinson Iredale, Edward's brother, transcribed it while it was still largely legible. There are gaps in it and unreadable entries which is not surprising. Overall, however, it gives a very graphic first hand impression of life in the trenches from the mundane to the horrific. He also wrote a diary in 1914, the year the war started and the original of that document survives. The 1914 diary is summarised in this publication.

The diaries become all the more poignant at the centenary of Edward's death in 2016 - the year this publication was created. This book is dedicated to the memory of Edward Iredale, Charles Iredale and the other men of Tadcaster who laid down their lives in the Great War.

Mark and Jeremy Swinden
Tadcaster
2016

Introduction

Four brothers, all born in Tadcaster, Yorkshire, served their country in the Great War. Two, Alfred Iredale and William Wilkinson Iredale, returned home and subsequently married and started families. Charles Iredale died in Bulgaria of pneumonia aged 25. Edward Elisha Iredale was killed in action in France aged 19.

This book is the story of Edward and is based around the diary he recorded of his experiences in the trenches during the First World War in 1915, often referred to as the Great War, and the diary he kept in 1914, the year that the Great War broke out.

Company Sergeant Major by the age of 19 and a recipient of the Military Medal, he served with bravery and distinction and lost his life in battle.

He is buried in Connaught Cemetery in Thiepval, France.

We have put this publication together based on a transcript of the original War Diary made by our late mother Betty, the daughter of William.

The 1914 diary had been preserved by the sister of the four brothers, the late Emmeline who had passed it on to her daughter Mary who has made it available to us for this publication. We are obliged to her, her son Peter and daughter Rachael for supplying various items, and for keeping alive the memory of our mutual family members.

Family Background

Charlie Iredale, a postman, or letter carrier as they were originally known, was born in Longwood near Huddersfield, Yorkshire on 27th September 1862. Amelia Wilkinson was born in Ouston Ferry in Lincolnshire on 26th December 1864.

Having moved to Tadcaster, they were married at the Wesleyan Chapel on the 26th March 1889. The Reverend E.F. Hardwick performed the ceremony.

They had a grand total of 12 children, the first one, Martha, being born in Otley. All the others were born in Tadcaster and all at home, as was the norm at the time, the majority at Drake's House, Chapel Street.

One child, unnamed, died soon after birth on 17th December 1892.

Everard, born 11th May 1906, died aged 8 months.

Of the ten who reached adulthood, four served in the Great War:

<u>William Wilkinson Iredale</u> Sapper Royal Engineers, survived but contracted malaria which affected him in subsequent years.

<u>Alfred Iredale</u> 2nd Lieutenant, who served in the Royal Flying Corps which subsequently became the Royal Air Force. He survived.

<u>Charles Iredale</u> Private, who served in the Royal Army Medical Corps and died of pneumonia on the 22nd October 1918. He

is buried in the Doiran Military Cemetery in Greece. He died in Strumitsa, Bulgaria and was 25 years of age.

Edward Elisha Iredale Company Sergeant Major, West Yorkshire Regiment, recipient of the Military Medal. He died in action in France on the 29th August 1916 and was buried in the Connaught Cemetery, Thiepval, France. He was two months away from his 20th birthday.

Before the War, Edward had worked at John Smith's Brewery. Tadcaster, because of the limestone basin on which it sits has been famous as a brewing town for many years. In 1914 the three breweries in operation employed hundreds of local people before the days of automation.

John Smith's	now owned by Heineken UK
Samuel Smith's	still independent
The Tower Brewery	now owned by Molson Coors

William

Alfred

Charles

Edward

TSR.9   Bridge Street, TADCASTER.   Copyright Frith

Tadcaster's main street with John Smith's Brewery
prominent, early in the last century

Diary 1914

As a precursor to the main war diary kept by Edward in 1915, another diary which he kept for the previous year gives an impression of life in the lead-up to the hostilities. Many of the entries are quite brief and give the details of the life of a 17 year old lad living in Tadcaster and working at John Smith's Brewery.

Edward was interested in football and boxing and he gives details of local football results and professional boxing matches as well as games and sparring sessions he had taken part in. He enjoyed typical country pursuits of the time such as bird nesting and following the hounds. He attended chapel and classes every Sunday and was attending night school three times a week.

The 1914 diary can be read, with the benefit of hindsight, as falling into 3 phases. The first part of the year up to April 1914 gives the day by day details of peacetime life in Tadcaster. The second phase covers the period from when Edward is accepted into the territorials in May until the declaration of war on 4th August which was the day that Edward's unit received orders to mobilise. The third part is the period in training after that date.

January – April 1914

This part of the diary is characterised by brief notes entered virtually every day, and weeks that followed a pattern, as would be the case for all working people.

Edward attended night school on Monday, Tuesday and Thursday most weeks. We do know that he was studying Shorthand, English, Arithmetic, Commercial Practice and French. He attended the Methodist Church every Sunday and he notes the names of the preachers. Saturdays were often devoted to sport, either football or boxing with his friends. We know from some football team formations noted in the diary that he played on the left wing. He only weighed 8 stone 12 pounds and was presumably pretty quick and skilful as he scored a lot of goals.

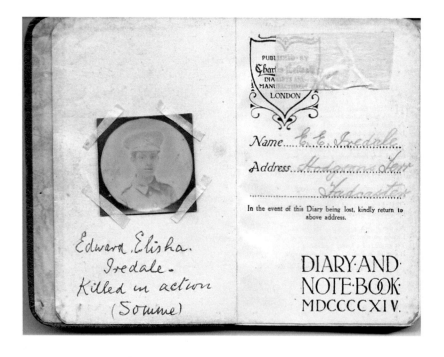

These various facets of Edward's life can be seen from some of the more interesting entries in his diary: preface illustrated above.

January

Friday 2nd
Won rabbit in raffle.

Monday 5th
3rd in Christmas exam at evening school.

Wednesday 14th
Had day off to follow foxhounds. Met at Grimston Park. Killed 1 at Toulston. Concert in aid of Children's home.

Saturday 24th
Played Bramham at Bramham lost 9-1 .

Saturday 31st
Played Grammar School. Lost 6-2 Scored 1 goal. Father taken ill.

February

Edward noted that father was off work every day until he returned to work on 18th by which time Edward's brother William was also ill and off work.

He continues to record his attendance at evening school, chapel, and sports noting on Saturday 28th February that *"Tad won Boston 8-0."* His friend A Lofthouse started work in the Brewery cellar on Monday 23rd.

March

His father and brother William were both off work for the first half of March. Entries for the early part of the month show his interest in boxing .

Monday 2nd
Gave 6d towards boxing gloves for Catholic rooms.

Wednesday 4th
Wells beat Blake in 4 rounds.

Monday 9th
Boxed A Hawkins.

Tuesday 10th
New boxing gloves came.

This was also examination time. Edward took exams in Commercial Practice on Thursday 26th, English on Monday 30th, and Shorthand on 31st. He also noted on Saturday 28th that *"Tad beat Malton 13-0"*

April

With the arrival of Spring, we find Edward on a *"wend round Rudgate"* on Wednesday 1st, finding *"2 golf balls on riverside"* on Saturday 4th and running – *"Ran round Stutton with A Birdsall in 20 Minutes"* on Friday 24th. There was plenty of football going on and Edward scored a goal in an 8-2 victory on Monday 13th (Easter Monday) and 2 goals in game on Monday 27th when Hop Squeezers played Tub Fillers and won 4 -1 – these are obviously informal brewery teams.

Evening classes had finished but Edward attended chapel every Sunday. The lesson on Sunday 5th was Jesus washing his disciples' feet.

Two entries point the way to the next phase.

Tuesday 21st
A Lofthouse passed for Territorials.

Wednesday 29th
Dr Glover passed me as fit for Territorials.

May – July 1914

During these months the emphasis moves quite rapidly from a civilian life in Tadcaster to a life dominated by military drills and associated activities.

May

Edward notes the cricket scores every Saturday and also went bird nesting a few times. This was a popular – and legal – pastime in those days. However the entries for the first few days show what is in store.

Friday 1st
Went to Terriers supper.

Monday 4th
Went to York with A Lofthouse to get Terriers clothes.

Tuesday 5th
First drill in Terriers room.

Friday 8th
Drill.

Sunday 10th
Military Sunday. Went to York with Terriers.

Tuesday 12th
Drill.

Friday 15th
First field drill.

The entry for Thursday 28th is interesting
Bought rifle off Metcalfe for 1/6.

June

The month of June is dominated by drills including Edward's first trip to Strensall Army Base on Saturday 13th where he notes. *"Got 2 bulls out of 5".*

Still working full time at this point, his spare time was spent nesting and fishing and he was attending chapel every Sunday - for example on Sunday 7th where the lesson was David killing Goliath.

July

July starts with an entry on Wednesday 1st
"Had the heaviest storm seen by anyone living at Tadcaster."

The first part of the month was more of the same – drills, chapel on Sundays, boxing – Edward *"boxed E Atkinson & H Varley on sands"* on Wednesday 8th

On Friday 24th Edward had his last field drill before camp and spent the next day getting ready for camp – which was in Scarborough. His entries for the remainder of the month describe the regime at camp.

Sunday 26th
Started at 4.30 am arrived Scarboro 8.30 am. Got blankets and beds. Bed at 10 pm.

Monday 27th
Up at 4 am. Biscuits & Coffee at 5.30 am Adju parade 6.00 am Breakfast 7.30 am Cols parade 8.45 am Rifle inspection 9 am Bed at 10 pm.

Tuesday 28th
Up at 5 am Biscuits & coffee 5.30 Ad parade 6. Breakfast 7.30 Colonel parade 8.45 am Rifle inspection. Bed at 10 pm.

Wednesday 29th
Same as yesterday, Dress parade. Foot inspection.

Thursday 30th
Same as yesterday. A & B Companies on night outpost from 8 pm to 4 am.

Friday 31st

No adjuds parade for A & B. Payday 8/-.
Memo. Colonels parade & manoeuvres from 8.45 am to 2 pm
everyday.

August – December 1914

August

Edward was still in camp at the start of August. War was
declared on 4th August and Edward's unit was mobilised on
that day as the diary reflects.

Sunday 2nd
Food whilst at Scarbro. Breakfast bacon & coffee. Dinner meat

potatoes peas. Tea butter jam & bread, tea.

Monday 3rd Bank Holiday
Got order to pack all up ready to go to Tadcaster. Slept in Drill hall York at night. I was on guard in Scarbro station.

Tuesday 4th
Arrived in Tad 8 am. Got orders to mobilise and go to York. Slept at home.

Wednesday 5th
Started for York 7.30 am, Arrived in York 8.30 am.

Thursday 6th –Saturday 8th
Sleeping in Drill Hall at York.

On August 10th the unit moved to Selby and *"pitched tents in wrong field"*. In between guard duty and drills Edward went to the Globe picture house on 13th and Central picture house on 14th, by which time they had moved to the correct field. They were there for 9 days before moving to York.

Sunday 16th
Waggonette party came from Tadcaster.

Monday 17th
Went in baths with A Lofthouse. Route march with full packs on. About 5 miles.
Memo. Food whilst at Selby. Breakfast Jam & bread. Dinner meat & potatoes. Tea Jam & bread.

Wednesday 19th
Started for York 12.30 am. Arrived in York 1 pm.

The period in York was mainly drills and route marches.
After attending Church parade and Wesleyan parade on
Sunday 23rd, Edward walked to Tadcaster and then returned
by train having walked to Bolton (Percy) station. He had a visit
from his parents and another trip home before moving to
Strensall Army Base on 31st.

Saturday 29th
*Mother & Father came to York. Saw two aeroplanes flying over
Knavesmire.*

Sunday 30th
Went to Tadcaster. Cycled there walked back to Bolton.

Monday 31st
*Marched to Strensall. Left York 8.30 am. Arrived in Strensall at
11.00 am.*

September

The whole of September was spent in Strensall doing drills and
route marches – punctuated by two trips to Tadcaster.
Edward managed a trip home on Sunday 13th – by walking
to York, cycling to Tadcaster, then cycling back to York and
catching a train, and another on Saturday 26th.
He volunteered for foreign service – it had never been
expected that the Territorials would see service overseas.

Wednesday 2nd
Volunteered for foreign service. Route march 8 miles.

Wednesday 16th
Said I was 19 & got passed for foreign service. [He was 17]

Thursday 17th
Got innoculated in left arm. Rain all day no parade.

Friday 18th
Arm stiff slight pain in head. No parade for us. Pay day. 7/-

Saturday 19th
Colour Sergeant Birkbeck married. No parade for us. Alfred & Frank Thornton came. Arm stiff.
Memo. Food at Strensall. Breakfast Bacon & Tea.
Dinner meat roast & stew on alternate days potatoes & carrots or turnips. Tea Cheese & Jam & bread.

Sunday 20th
Arm still a little stiff.

Tuesday 29th
Got innoculated again. Got off parades. M Franklin got married.

October

Edward came home to Tadcaster on Thursday 1st until Saturday when he returned to Strensall. The Unit moved to Selby on Saturday 10th before returning to Strensall the following Saturday and then moving to York the Saturday after that (24th) where they were billeted at the Railway Institute. It was Edward's 18th Birthday on Sunday 18th and he went to Strensall Church.
He had a visit from his Father and brother Alfred the following day.
He noted that it was his brother Charlie's 21st birthday on Wednesday 21st. [Charlie died on active service in Bulgaria in 1918]

He managed another trip home and a little entertainment.

Sunday 25th
Cycled to Tadcaster. Got wet through coming back.

Monday 26th
Went to Opera.

Tuesday 27th
Went to Bostocks & Wombwells menagerie.

The unit was still at Strensall on the last day of the month, and Edward managed another brief visit home.

November

November started quietly. Edward managed a 24 hour trip home on Sunday 8th, a trip to the pictures and two to the Opera, when not on military duty which consisted mainly of *"trenching"*.

On Thursday 12th the unit moved to Harrogate for a few days.

Thursday 12th
Went to Harrogate 1.40 train.

Friday 13th
Pay day 7/-. Went to pictures at Kursaal.

Sunday 15th
Snowed nearly all day.

Monday 16th

Firing at Burton Crag range. Went to Empire at night.

Tuesday 17th

Marking for B company. Came back to York 11 pm.

Edward had an afternoon back in Tadcaster on Saturday 28th which he notes was his sister Emmeline's birthday.

December

Entries in the diary become briefer in December during which time the unit was still in York. There were two trips home in between routine military duties. The last two entries in the 1914 diary are these:

Monday 21st

William & P Morley joined Royal Engineers and Grenadier Guards.

Tuesday 22nd

Brigade day 8.30 am to 4 pm.

[William was Edward's eldest brother – he served in Salonika, the same theatre of war as Charlie, and survived the war.]

Enlistment and Deployment to France

Edward Elisha Iredale enlisted in the 5th Battalion of the Prince of Wales' Own West Yorkshire Regiment in Tadcaster in May 1914. This was shortly before the start of the First World War and the battalion was one of four forming the 1st West Riding Brigade of the West Riding (Territorial) Division. This later became the 146th Brigade of the 49th (West Riding) Division.

The territorial units were comprised of volunteers who were under no obligation to serve overseas. After the outbreak of war on 4th August 1914, territorials were given the option of serving overseas and by the end of August over 70 battalions had volunteered, including the 5th which was concentrated at Selby on 10th August. As more battalions were raised, the original ones were given the designation "1", so Edward's battalion became the 1/5th. Initial training took place at Strensall and in York. This was followed by a period on the Lincolnshire coast.

Edward's Great War diary starts on Thursday 15th April 2015 when the brigade had departed from Gainsborough with the rest of the division, bound for France.

The Western Front

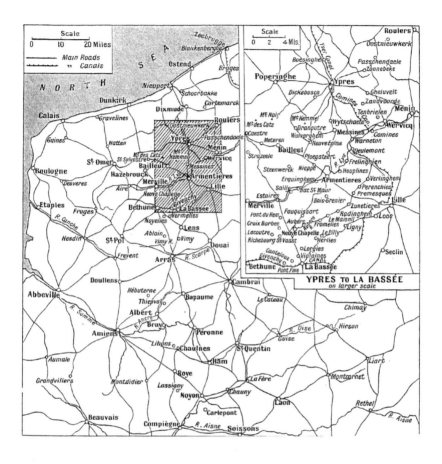

April 1915

Thursday 15th

We left Gainsboro. where we had been staying about a week
and took the early afternoon train to Folkestone by way of
Cambridge, London and then through Kent. We had a few
minutes in London and most of us took the opportunity of getting
something to eat.
Most of us were impressed by the scenery in Kent and also by the
hop gardens and large orchards.
Our boat was waiting for us at Folkestone and we embarked and
in a very little time we were landed in Boulogne.

Friday 16th

We left our camp which was on a high hill near Boulogne and
walked about 4 miles to Pontebrigge Station, the heat of the
march was awful and we were glad to buy oranges at 1d each
from the French vendors who followed us nearly all the way.
At the station we were put in cattle trucks, 43 each and in this
manner we travelled to Merville where we disembarked and
marched to La Sart. Here we were put in an old barn for the
night and right glad we were to get there.

Saturday 17th

We woke up about 7am after a heavy and cramped sleep of about
6 hours and made breakfast of biscuits and bully beef (bread not
being at present in our ration and being 8d a cake to buy). Red
and white wine can be bought here for 2d a glass and beer 1d a
glass but the beer is only very light and mostly home brewed. I
should say the gravity is about 5.

Aeroplanes are very common round here and we soon cease to take notice of them except when we think there are signs of a scrap.

Sunday 18th

This is our first Sunday in France but the day of rest is no longer such as we soon find out when we have to go on a 10 mile route march in the blazing sun. The want of English cigarettes and tobacco is keenly felt by those who have not prepared and French tobacco and cigs are indulged in with disastrous results. We find that the French peasants round here do not give much thought to sanitation and drainage but put this down to one of the results of war.

Monday 19th

We were moved from this billet owing to it's overcrowded state and put in a barn about 2 miles away and I am sure we appreciated the change. This billet is on the edge of a big wood into which we often went to get our meals (such as they were). These days were our happiest in France. We can hear the big guns booming all day and night and, when it is dark, we can see the lights which are used for the purpose of locating any enemy working parties or patrols. The billet is 5 miles from the firing line.

Redeployment to Ypres

This section of the diary ends on Monday 19th April and recommences on Sunday 1st August 1915.

At the start of this period the troops were based at Merville in France. They were deployed to a number of front line locations in the vicinity of Neuve Chapelle. There were no significant attacks on the trenches by either side, but there was frequent shelling, mortar and sniper fire. There were a number of casualties during this period.

July 1915 saw the West Yorkshire Regiment deployed to the part of the front line at Ypres and on the 6th of that month they marched to Poperinge, a town about 7 miles to the west of Ypres, and a significant gathering point for allied troops as it was the only Belgian town of any size that was still behind allied lines. They were billeted at Coppernolle, about 2 miles north of Poperinge. The following day, 7th July, the 1/5th and 1/7th West Yorkshires relieved other troops of the Division and occupied a line of trenches about 2 miles North East of Ypres, in the vicinity of Turco Farm.

This new location was much more dangerous than the part of the line they had recently vacated and came under bombardment shortly after it had been occupied. In the next few days there was a great deal of enemy action including from gas shells, which were fired as part of an attack by the enemy on 10th July. There was a counter attack by the King's Own Yorkshire Light Infantry which recaptured trenches which had been temporarily taken. The whole line was bombarded again on 13th July.
There was constant gunfire and shelling.

On 31st July the 1/5th relieved the 1/6th Battalion and took over dug-outs on the bank of the Yser Canal, one mile north of Ypres.

Edward's diary recommences the following day.

August

Sunday 1st

Cpl. Tuppen was shot in the back of the head and killed. He had been looking over the parapet for about half a minute when he turned his back to the enemy and stood talking to Harold Simpson. Whilst thus occupied he was spotted by a German and shot.

[AD Tuppen is commemorated on the Menin Gate, Ypres]

Quartermaster Dobson wounded.

Lance Cpl. Bradley came back to our platoon and took charge of Cpl. Tuppen's section.

I was Cpl. over (the) listening post (Pte Fry and Pte Terry) we did half an hour out and an hour in until "stand to".

Monday 2nd

We were subjected to a heavy trench mortar bombardment and had 2 men killed. We were then ordered to withdraw into the communication (trench) and told that the artillery would bombard the enemy's mortar position but after being in the trench half an hour, we were sent back, no bombardment having taken place.

Our position in the line is about 400 yards on the left of our previous front line position and we are about 100 yards from German lines.

Our platoon did not supply (a) listening post.

Tuesday 3rd

Last night a party of wire menders who were in front of the trenches came across three Germans laid just in front of our wire. The Germans showed fight but were soon overpowered and brought in and afterwards gave some useful information.

The position here is regarded as a dangerous one and so we keep our bayonets fixed all day and stand to from 9 at night until 3.30 in the morning when we are relieved by the platoon in reserve.

Wednesday 4th

Today is the anniversary of the War and it is supposed that the Kaiser will make his final dash for Calais today or tonight and so we are thoroughly prepared for anything that may happen and we are all anticipating an attack although we know that the enemy cannot hope to break our lines at this point owing to the strength of the position, but instead of the attack, we had one of the quietest days we have experienced in this part of the line.

Thursday 5th

We were bombarded with trench mortars just after stand to and one of the howitzer section was killed.

We were also heavily bombarded with mortars at about 5 at night, our casualties being 1 killed and 2 wounded.
This is the heaviest trench mortar bombardment I have ever experienced and many of our chaps had their nerves completely shattered by the terrific explosions.

No listening post was sent out at night.

Friday 6th

We were ordered to retire into the communication trench on our left owing to enemy trench mortars and, whilst we were there, our artillery dropped a few shells on the German trenches causing damage which kept the enemy at work during the day.

We were relieved by the 6th West Yorks at about 11pm and we landed down the far side of the Yser canal about 12pm. We found there 9 reinforcements from Havre, C. Atkinson being among them.

Saturday 7th

I was on R E fatigue to the 8th West Yorks who were occupying the front line trenches. Our stores were dropped in the reserve trenches and were carried there to the line by the 8th.

The day was fairly quiet and there was very little firing.
Our food whilst we were here was very good and plentiful and the

reserves who joined us here were favourably impressed by the fare.

A few shells were dropped in the village of Vlamertinge.

Sunday 8th

I was Orderly Corporal and was found plenty to do.

Our artillery bombarded the enemy front line area at intervals during the day.

There is here the grave of Lieut. Briggs of the 7th West Yorks. (Leeds Rifles). He is the son of F. D. Briggs, a Director for Messrs J. Smiths and his grave is situated about 70 yards on the right of my dug-out. The cross on it is very good, being composed of white wood.

Lieutenant Briggs

Lieutenant Richard Stanley Briggs of the 7th Battalion West Yorkshire Regiment (Leeds Rifles) had been killed on 29th July 1915, at the age of 20.

His final resting place is Essex Farm Cemetery by the canal bank at Ypres, close to the location of the medical post which is behind the front line.

The grave which Edward mentions would have been where Lieutenant Briggs had fallen, 11 days earlier, on the front line. John Smith's was (and still is, in its modern form) a major brewery in Tadcaster. Edward had worked there prior to enlisting, and seeing the grave would have been a poignant moment for him.

Monday 9th and Tuesday 10th

Reveille at 7am.

Following last night's bombardment, the Infantry attacked in the Hooge district, their object being to straighten the line at that point.

They achieved their object and captured some lines of trenches and hundreds of prisoners, many of whom passed through Vlamertinge on the way to the internment camps.

The condition of these prisoners was much talked about by those who saw them. These men said they were either old men or young boys who looked as though they had had no substantial food for weeks and their condition in general was deplorable. There was intermittent artillery fire on both sides during the day.

Pte. Lamplow was made L. Cpl.

L. Cpl H Atkinson was made Corporal.

My pay as Lance Corporal commenced from this date.

Wednesday 11th

Sgt. Pickering was stripped by District Court Martial for being drunk on duty and sentenced as a Private to 3 months first field punishment. He transferred to C Company.

Aeroplanes were active all day.

One of our airmen attacked an enemy aeroplane and apparently wounded the airman or partly disabled the machine, the airman making for enemy lines in sinking condition.

Fred Boynton came back from hospital.
Colonel Wood went to hospital.

Pte Storey made unpaid L. Cpl.

Thursday 12th

Cpl. Banton's birthday, 21 years.

Enemy shelled canal with small shell during the day and also they fired large shells at St. Jean.

Usual artillery fire on our side.

A Clarke (reserve) left us, bad feet. H Hawkins came back from bombing.

Capt. Mackay went into hospital.

We relieved the 6th West Yorks in front line trenches on the immediate left of our last front line trench. It is supposed to be an advanced trench, it runs at an angle of 75 degrees and is rather hot.

Friday 13th

Stand to until 3.30 am, double sentries until 7 am owing to fog.

Contrary to our expectations, the day was very quiet and uneventful.

The Germans on our front seem to be a very quiet lot, probably our success on the right and the occasional co-operation of our artillery account for this.

We had no water ration issued and so we drank the water from water holes which are fairly abundant in these trenches.
We stood to at 8.30pm until 3.15am with fixed bayonets as usual.

Saturday 14th

We got our first water ration at 4pm, half a bottle of water per man.

A Cowan (reserve) was wounded in the hand with a piece of shell. This was one of our own shells which burst in the German lines 80 yards away.

The bombers supplied 2 bombing posts in this trench, one at each end.

Whilst hunting for wood with F Terry, I came across 3 French soldiers partially buried with earth thrown up by a large shell or a trench mortar. They were decomposed and had evidently been there some time.

[Fred Terry was Edward's cousin who was in the same battalion. He died on 29th September 1916 and is commemorated on the Thiepval Memorial.]

Sunday 15th

Usual stand to, 9pm until 3.30 am.

Our artillery shelled the enemy's lines with high explosives and the enemy retaliated by shelling the Leeds rifles on our left, killing and wounding 17 men.

Our stretcher bearers were sent for to help with the cases and whilst S. B. Abbott was carrying wounded with a Leeds stretcher bearer, the Leeds S. B. was shot through the head and killed. Our lines are connected to the Leeds lines by an unoccupied trench about 100 yards long.

Monday 16th

The enemy located our working party at about 1 am, a burst of rapid fire for about 10 minutes being the result. Fortunately no-one was hit.
I might here mention that the Germans opposing us at this point appear to be well stocked with munitions of every kind, especially trench mortars, which are sent over at every attempt of our artillery or trench mortar.

These mortars are far superior to ours in every respect and I have seen them fire one over a distance of nearly 300 yards.

Tuesday 17th

Our trench howitzer battery opened fire just after stand to, firing 5 mortars. Only 3 of these burst. The enemy immediately replied with their more effective mortars and all, except sentries, were withdrawn from our trench so that our artillery could open fire on the German trenches, which they did, causing some damage.

Sgt Bean was wounded in the right arm whilst walking along the frontline and left us for hospital at night.

Wednesday 18th

It rained heavily at about 1.30am causing the trenches to be very muddy. The enemy fired about a dozen trench mortars just after stand to but did no damage to speak of. Our artillery replied by bombarding their trench with high explosive shells, knocking down portions of their trenches. The Germans, not to be beaten, bombarded the Leeds lines with shells. During these actions, we were withdrawn.

We were relieved by the 6th West Yorks and went into the reserve dug-outs about half a mile away from the canal camps.

Thursday 19th

Reveille 8 am. Breakfast over at 9.
This position is about one mile from firing line at its nearest point and is in rifle range.

The enemy shelled front line trenches very heavily during the day, our artillery replied rather weakly.
Was Corporal of trench guard at night and aeroplane guard during the day.

Many stretcher cases were brought from the lines occupied by the 6th West Yorks, they having been caused chiefly by trench mortars and bullets.

Friday 20th

Reveille 6am.

Very few aeroplanes active until evening when enemy craft were much in evidence.

Sgt Major Birbeck went on leave.
Fred Boynton's birthday, 19 years old.

After coming off guard at 8pm, I had to go on ration fatigue to canal bank until 10.30pm.

Major Stoddart left the battalion, (?) taking his place.
The Germans shelled us during the day but did little damage.
They also shelled the front line trenches with better results.

Saturday 21st

Reveille 6am.
Swimming races were arranged by batt. to take place in the Yser. There was also a batt. sing song. Some of A1 company were allowed to go.

Aeroplanes fairly active.

Water whilst we were here was fairly scarce, it having to be fetched from the water carts on the far side of the Yser canal, consequently we were only allowed one water bottle per day.
Sgt Wood went on pass.

Pte Gilbert Wetherell was made Lce Corporal whilst we were here.

Sunday 22nd

Reveille 6am.
Battalion swimming races were held in the Yser canal.

The Brigadier presented the prizes.

A sing song was also held at night.

It was very warm and fine all day and aircraft were much in evidence. We counted as many as 10 of our own and enemy craft up at the same time. We also counted 7 observation balloons.

I was Cpl over fatigue for making protection for latrines and building up 4 dug-out fronts with sand bags to afford protection from shrapnel.

Monday 23rd

Reveille 6am.

The following was circulated among the troops today and was said to be official having come through the 6th Division: The Germans have attempted a landing north of Riga and the Russians, having caught them, have sunk 1 super dreadnought, 2 cruisers, 7 torpedo boat destroyers and all their landing boats which were conveying troops to shore.

During the evening, our artillery which were shelling the front line trenches, hit something which caused a fire of 20 minutes duration.

Tuesday 24th

Reveille 6.30am.

Packing up till 12pm.

We relieved the 8th West Yorks at 2pm in the front line. This is the first time we have relieved or have been relieved in the daytime. We came up one section at at a time with 5 minutes interval.

This position is about a mile on the left of our last position in the firing line.

The Leeds Rifles said the position had been quiet during their occupation.

Wednesday 25th

Stand to over at 3.30am.

The enemy fired a few trench mortars at our section of trench but fortunately they did not land in the trench owing to them not getting a long enough range.

We stand to in these trenches from 8pm until 4am and also do fatigues during those hours and in the daytime we cook our meals and sleep.

We get more rest in these trenches than we have done in any other front line trenches.

Thursday 26th

The Germans bombarded the Leeds Rifles on our right very heavily with trench mortars, aerial torpedoes and shells, a few of which caught our position but did no damage.
The Leeds Rifles were withdrawn into our trenches and therefore they did not suffer much only having 2 casualties, one man having his head blown off and another being severely wounded in the back. Both of these were caused by the same shell which burst on the parapet. Our artillery opened a very effective fire in return.

Friday 27th

I was Orderly Corporal and had to parade the sick at Headquarters in the first reserve line. This is the first time we have had Orderly Sergeants and an Orderly Corporal in the front line trench.

Water here was not very plentiful, only a quarter per day being allowed but we made it spin out with water from the water holes which was of a very doubtful nature, but we think that anything is better than nothing so we risk it and almost hope for a month in hospital.

Saturday 28th

We heard we have to come in this line again but our hopes are not fulfilled.

Sunday 29th

It rained very heavily during the morning and intermittently during the afternoon and night, causing us much discomfort in the trenches.

At night I was on listening post with J. Henderson (bomber) a man who was nervous for such work and so I let him take my place which was laid in a hole under the parapet and I took his place laid out against barbed wire.

The night was fairly quiet and uneventful.

Monday 30th

The day was spoilt by heavy rain during the morning and early afternoon and we thought that we were going to have a wet night but it cleared somewhat towards night when the - - West Yorks came to relieve us, it was fine although very cloudy.

We came out in platoons using a new communication we had dug during our stay in the front line and we landed on the canal bank at about 10.30 am, the battalion having suffered only 2 casualties during the 6 days on the front line.

Tuesday 31st

Reveille 8am.

We occupied the lower dug-outs on the right of No 4 bridge. I noticed today whilst finding shrapnel bullets to use in my catapult that the dug-outs we occupied from 14th to 19th of July are all knocked in by shell fire and are now not used by the troops.

I had a swim in the Yser canal and found that the water was much cleaner than I expected. I saw H. Marshall for the first time in France.

The Ypres Salient at night

A night scene showing three soldiers on the fire step of a trench, surprised by a brilliant star shell lighting up the view over the battlefield. On the left there is a flooded shell-hole, beyond which stand three other soldiers, overlooked by a woodland of tree stumps.

Paul Nash © IWM (art.IWM ART 1145)

September

Wednesday 1st

I got up at 5 to go ratting with a friend and we had some fine sport before breakfast.

A dry canteen was opened today on the canal bank and was greatly appreciated by the troops. The goods sold were of course all tinned, were very good and they were sold at reasonable prices.

The English and French guns were active during the early morning and also at night, the enemy reply was rather feeble.

Thursday 2nd

We had the usual 2 hours before breakfast.

I was unlucky enough to catch R. E. fatigues. We drew our picks and shovels at 8.15 pm and went up towards Algerian Cottage to dig but we were sent back owing to the rain. We got drenched and having no change, we either had to sleep in our wet clothes or take them off and be starved [cold] all night. I chose the latter and knew about it during the night.
The artillery took some light guns up to the reserve trenches (15lb).

Friday 3rd

Owing to our wet clothes and the heavy rain all day, we spent the day in light attire (shirt and overcoat) and kept in dug-outs.

About 40 pairs of rubber top boots came to A Company to be distributed to the NCOs and some of the men who made good use of them when we went into the trenches.

During the day, many dug-outs either fell in or got flooded and their occupants had to repair their dug-outs above us which had been shelled and previously condemned.

Saturday 4th

I was made ? Corporal and owing to the fact that we left this position tonight for the trenches, I had my hands full.

It rained very heavily at intervals during the day so those who had top boots were glad of them when we left for the trenches at 9pm.

The communication trench was in a very bad state and matters were worse when we reached our destination which was support to the fire trench. Nearly all the dug-outs had fallen in and so we spent the night in a very miserable condition.

Sunday 5th

Our dug-out, through which the rain had been pouring all night, fell in at about 7am and so we set on straight away to build another. This was no light task owing to the heavy rain but we managed to get shelter for ourselves before night.

I was on ration fatigue to the canal bank and by the time we had taken water to the front line trench and got back again, I was thoroughly done up but fortunately we were given a rum ration and so, after drinking my ration, I laid down and slept heavily until morning.

Monday 6th

I might here mention that although I was strictly teetotal before coming out here, I never refused my rum ration out here and I consider it is absolutely necessary as a stimulant and also as an inducement to sleep during the very cold nights.
We were building dug-outs and repairing the trenches all day. Fortunately the weather seems to have improved somewhat and we look like having a fine week.

The French intermittently bombarded the enemy positions with shrapnel and we received a few shells on our position in return.

Tuesday 7th

During the day we had a few shells on our position but no-one was hit. The French bombarded at intervals during the day and the Germans bombarded Ypres with large shells in the afternoon.

The French artillery seems to be very effective in this district and they always give the enemy more than he sends.

I was Corporal of the guard from 7.30pm until 4am when I was relieved by Corporal Moore.

Wednesday 8th
Unreadable

Thursday 9th
Unreadable

Friday 10th
Unreadable

Saturday 11th
Unreadable

Sunday 12th

A Church of England service was held in the wood and as there was no Wesleyan service, I went to the C of E service.

It was Fred's birthday today and so we had plenty of grub all day and for a few days after the event.

The French guns on our left have been very quiet lately as also have our guns on the right but the Allies anti-aircraft guns have been very active.

Monday 13th

I was crimed for being 2 minutes late on running parade. We were inspected by General Plumer at 12.30 am and he expressed his satisfaction with the Brigade.

The Tykes held a very good concert in the evening and they had a very large and appreciative audience.

Captain Mackay returned to the battalion and took charge of A Company.

Passes for Poperinghe are all owed at the rate of 2%?

Tuesday 14th

I was up at orderly charged with being 2 minutes late on running drill and I got off without being penalised. I was also evidence for

Mulrooney and Firth who were charged with missing parade.

It is now hop picking season and it is very interesting to watch the Belgian peasants picking the hop flowers and putting them into the large bags or pockets. Each farm appears to have a field of its own and the whole family turn out in force to pick the hops making a very picturesque sight.

Wednesday 15th

Reveille 6.30am.

A few of my pals and myself secured passes for Poperinghe from 4.30 to 9am and we had a very enjoyable time there.

Many English goods are sold in the town but are of course highly priced. Poperinghe has suffered slightly in one quarter from shells but otherwise the war has not had much effect on it, the only noticeable thing being the large number of deserted and closely shuttered houses.

Thursday 16th
Unreadable

Friday 17th
Unreadable

Saturday 18th
Unreadable

Sunday 19th

There was a Wesleyan parade in the morning near the Brigade headquarters.

At night, a few of my pals and myself went into the ? camp to see H. Briggs and on the way back came across some Belgian and Algerian soldiers who are billeted round here. All the Belgian soldiers are quiet and pleasant and they are always willing to help in any way.

Their chief occupation when not working seems to be making souvenirs out of shell cases and shell noses.

Monday 20th

We spent the morning and afternoon cleaning lines and at 7.30pm we marched off in platoons for the canal bank. Owing to the fact that the Germans are shelling High Street, we took a different route and marching through Brielen, we landed on the far bank of the canal at about 10pm.

We took over from K.O.Y.L.I. [King's Own Yorkshire Light Infantry] *who had left everything very dirty. Our position on the canal bank is on the left of our previous positions and is near the point where the canal bends to the river.*

Wednesday 22nd

Reveille 8am.

We had a very easy day, only having one fatigue to supply.

H. Briggs and C. Cawood came back to the battalion from the rest camp. Our artillery bombarded during the afternoon and the enemy put a few shells on the other side of the canal bank at night.

It was getting cold at nights but having had blankets brought up last night in our packs by the transport, we did not feel it very much.

It has been very clear all day and aircraft have been very active.

Thursday 23rd

During the morning the enemy bombarded our position with high explosives and wounded 3 of B Company.

There was some very heavy bombarding on our right (about a mile) by our artillery, the enemy replied rather feebly.

I have noticed whilst in this part of the line that the German way of exacting vengeance for our bombardments is to persistently shell farms in the vicinity of the firing line, or failing that, to shell the ruin of Ypres.

Friday 24th

The Germans dropped about half a dozen shells on our position, one of which hit the stays of our dug-out.

It was rumoured that the French had captured nearly 20 miles of trenches and were surrounding Lille and that the English had taken 12 miles.

Pte Hardwick was hit in the shoulder with a bullet.

Saturday 25th

More successes on our right.
We stood to from 5.30 to 6.30 am owing to our artillery

bombardment, the Germans replied rather feebly.

Large bombing parties took bombs up to the front line and bombed the enemy lines. This gave the enemy the idea that we were going to attack at this quarter, they therefore brought up their reserve force, weakening their position on the right where the real attack was made.

Sunday 26th

Lieut. Lee (who had just come out of hospital) accidently shot himself through the finger with his revolver.

One of our airmen, whilst circling over enemy lines, was attacked by 3 of their aeroplanes. He fought gamely and tried to reach our lines but, being outnumbered, he could not manage this and was eventually brought down about 300 yards in rear of the German lines.

We left the canal bank about 7pm relieved by the 8th in front line.

Monday 27th

Father's birthday, also H. Marshall.

Our position at present is slightly on the right of our former front line position.

The state of the trenches is, on the whole, fairly good but most of the dug-outs are very badly built and they are also insufficient meaning more work for us.
The allies bombarded heavily during the night causing the enemy

to open a heavy fire.
Bombing was continued by both sides, practically all night, on our left.

Tuesday 28th

During the morning our Colonel caused an oilsheet to be put out in the sap informing our enemy of our captures. The enemy immediately bombarded the sap with shells, trench mortars, rifle grenades and bombs. Then a small party of the enemy rushed into our sap, bayoneted one man and took the sheet but not without loss.

Our casualties for the day, 8.

Cecil Yates shot through the head.

[C Yates is buried at Essex Farm Cemetry]

Pioneer Hudson accidently shot through the leg by Sandbrook.

Wednesday 29th

It rained heavily all night and day causing the trenches and dug-outs (most of which were waterlogged) to be in a very bad condition.

We stand to in this part of the line from 6.30 until 7 am and from 4.45 until 5.15 pm.

The village of Pilkem, which can be seen plainly on our left, was bombarded.

October

Friday 8th

We spent the day cleaning up billets.
We marched off from canal bank at about 7.30 pm and arrived
in the support dug-out at about 8.15pm where we relieved the 8th
West Yorks.

Our position here is about 100 yards from the front line.
Our dug-outs are very good, in fact they are the best dug-outs we
have been in yet.

One of the 8th West Yorks was killed and one wounded at the rail
head.

Saturday 9th

The enemy fired the usual number of shells on canal bank.

The aeroplanes of both sides were active all day.

The Germans use their machine guns very freely round here and
sometimes very effectively as one chap (with 5 bullets through his
shoulder) would be able to prove.

A few trench mortars and rifle grenades were fired on the front
line without doing much damage.

Sunday 10th

Very heavy gunfire was heard all last night and it appeared to
come from the Hooge district.

Cpl Storey was wounded in head.

Sgt. Daffy, C. Company was wounded also Lieut Brown, B Company.

I was on Headquarters fatigue from 9 am until 5 pm.

I witnessed 3 aeroplane fights, the enemy planes being driven off twice and ours once.

A few whizz bangs were fired on our position, no one hit.
L. Cpl E. Atkinson was made full Cpl. dating back a fortnight.

Monday 11th

H. Briggs was made L. Cpl and I was put in orders as paid dating from 19th June.

An enemy plane whilst being shelled by our pom-poms fell down an air pocket turning over about 2 dozen times, he eventually righted the plane and flew away to the enemy lines.

The enemy bombarded the canal bank, our lines and the front line, one or two casualties sustained. Some shells fell in Brielen catching some artillery which was moving. 13 men were hit and 10 horses killed.

Tuesday 12th

The enemy shelled the position held by the left half of our platoon. One shell dropped in the machine gunners dug-out, wounded 2 men.
The canal bank was also very heavily shelled.

Very heavy artillery fire could be heard nearly all day from the right, probably Loos.

Several of our chaps were suffering from shock owing to the heavy bombardment. Many shells dropped near dug-outs and failed to explode.

Wednesday 13th

Our artillery shelled the enemy front line during the afternoon and we also fired many trench mortars breaking their lines in many places. The enemy replied and kept up an intermittent bombardment all the afternoon. Some shells caught the West Riding at Follina farm, a whole platoon was wounded.

Between the 14th and 21st the Battalion were in reserve in Coppernolle.

Thursday 21st

We went for a bath at 8 am.

We left the camp at about 5 pm and set off with a full pack (including blanket and oilsheet) for the trenches, a distance of about 8 miles. We were almost knocked when we landed about 7.30 pm. We relieved the Leicesters in the support trenches.

I was on duty straight away and was on until 6pm on Wednesday. F. Terry joined us at No. 4 bridge.

It was very cold during the night and we were glad of the extra underclothing we brought.

Friday 22nd

I was on duty until 6 pm.
We stood to from 4.40 until 5.30.
The enemy shelled spasmodically all day causing a good deal of harm to the trenches and regiments on our right.

A great many of the German shells are dud, especially the large range shells, more than half of which do not explode.

E. Firth went to hospital.

Our position here is just on the right of the road leading to No. 4 bridge and we are about half a mile from the front line.

Saturday 23rd

Stand to 5.30 to 6 am.
It was very cold during the night and nearly all day.

The enemy guns bombarded at intervals during the day and our guns replied occasionally.

F. Terry put in application for leave.

Our position here is about half a mile from the front line and we are slightly on the right of Duck's Bill.

Our aeroplanes were active all day.

These trenches are very well constructed and they were also very clean when we took over.

YPRES. — Le Nieuwerck avant et après le Bombardement.
The Nieuwerk before the Bombardment and after.

Visé Paris N° 270615-8   Photo ANTONY. Ypres.

Postcard of Ypres sent home by Edward in November 1915

Sunday 24th

I went on duty at 6 am until 6 pm.
Our artillery was active nearly all the day and also during the evening, the enemy guns only fired occasionally.

We were relieved at 6.30 pm and marched up to the firing line relieving the 8th West Yorks who had had a very rough time with shells.

The men were on duty until 6 am when it was almost daylight. It was very cold during the night.

Monday 25th

We stood to at 5.15 until 6 am.

It rained practically all day and night.

November

Wednesday 10th

Cpls E. and H. Atkinson made Sgt.

Cpl. Banton got his commission.

These men also got commissions; Sgt Major Birbeck, Cpl. Birbeck, Sgt. Gaunt, Sgt. Witton.

Monday 22nd

Whilst out on platoon between the lines, Bomber Knowles was fatally wounded and I was slightly hit with a German bomb.

E. Firth and myself got Knowles in.

[J H Knowles is buried at Lijssenthoek Military Cemetery]

Tuesday 23rd

I came from Essex Farm to 3rd West Riding Field Hospital.

Thursday 25th

Came down in train from Casualty Clearing Station to Boulogne and then by car to No 14 General Hospital.

Saturday 27th

Was operated on in the morning, 3 pieces being taken out of my leg. I was under chloroform.

Sunday 28th

Hot formentations put on my leg until the 2nd December.

Monday 29th

I was allowed up.

December

Thursday 2nd

I was put under X ray and another piece of bomb was found in my leg.

Friday 3rd

Underwent another operation (cocaine being used) and the piece was extracted and another two stitches put in.

Sunday 5th

One stitch taken out.

Monday 6th

One stitch taken out and I was marked for England.

Tuesday 7th

Hot dressings put on until I left.

Ypres 1915

Wounded British soldiers, swathed in bandages and lying on stretchers, are in the process of being moved onto two waiting motor ambulances by orderlies of the Royal Army Medical Corps. The vehicles are on the left and some of the ruined buildings of Ypres are visible on the right.

Gilbert Rogers © IWM (art.IWM ART 3792)

Return to the Front Line

There are no more entries in the diary following Edward's injury and repatriation. However, by early Summer 1916 he had returned to the front line.

The four territorial battalions had been withdrawn from Ypres late in December 1915 and by the middle of January were in training near Calais.

On 2nd February 1916 the Infantry Brigade arrived at Longeau near Amiens and by 12th February two battalions (1/6th and 1/8th) were positioned in front line trenches with the 1/7th and 1/5th in support and reserve respectively. The line ran east of Thiepval Wood in a large area known as the Somme.

Edward's letter to his mother mentions the first attack on 1st July which he missed.

This first attack was the ill fated attack on Thiepval, at the start of the Somme Offensive which would become the largest action in which the British Army had participated in history, to that date. The results of the events on the 1st and 2nd July were chaos, confusion and above all carnage on an unimaginable scale. Success in military terms was negligible. On 1st July alone over 19,000 British troops lost their lives and twice that number suffered serious injuries. The action continued in the form of specific attacks and local fighting until November.

The attack on 20th July was primarily made by the 1/8th Battalion and presumably Edward had been attached to that brigade as he had missed (and therefore survived) the battle on 1st July.

His last writing is a letter to his mother dated 22nd and 26th July 1916.

West Yorkshire Regiment Cap Badge

France 22nd July 1916

Dear Mother,

I hope you will not be angry with me for not writing before this but we have had such an exciting time this last month and my new duties take up so much of my time that I have had very little time for myself.

Since I last wrote, we have been in two attacks, the first on July 1st. I was not allowed to take part and I think it was best for me although I was aching to be in it, because it was not a success and every Sgt. in my Company except one was destined to be either wounded or killed, so also were our officers.

The second attack, which we made on July 20th was the most glorious and exciting day I have ever experienced and during that day I stood in the first German trench that has been captured by our Brigade since we came out.

It was the greatest honour I have been permitted to take part in, to stand in a trench which we ourselves captured from the Prussian Guards and to see the wounded Germans laid about with our chaps bandaging them, dead Germans blown to bits with our bombs and the remainder on the retreat. Some of our chaps were building barricades, some were still bombing the retreating Germans, the remainder were collecting souvenirs. Helmets were being carried away , bayonets, overcoats, razors, German buttons, bombs etc, all were picked and either kept or thrown away according to their value. I got a German officer's overcoat which I have yet and am going to sell, also a German bomber's or sniper's tassle which I took off the bayonet of a wounded German and a Prussian Guard's button and a German cap badge which I am sending you. Fred got a beautiful little

*safety razor and Bobby (our pal) got a souvenir in the shape
of a smashed wrist from an explosive bullet. Altogether we had
an exciting time and did not lose many men. We could have got
German rifles and bayonets but we cannot get them home and we
may be called to do our bit again at any minute. Our chaps are
even selling splendid German helmets for about 10 or 15 shillings.*

Continued 26th July 1916

*I am sending this letter and the tassle and cap badge to Mrs
Atkinson along with some of Eddie Atkinson's effects. The
German button I have lost.*

*We are going back into the trenches tomorrow morning but don't
worry. Fred is now acting Sgt. and I am acting Coy. Sgt Major so
please address my letters Act Coy Sgt Major in future.*

*I will send my card from the general as soon as I can get it
through.*

*Now I must close, hoping you are all quite well at home. Please
let my friends know that I am alright and don't bother about me,
there are thousands of others, just keep smiling.*

Your affectionate son

Edward

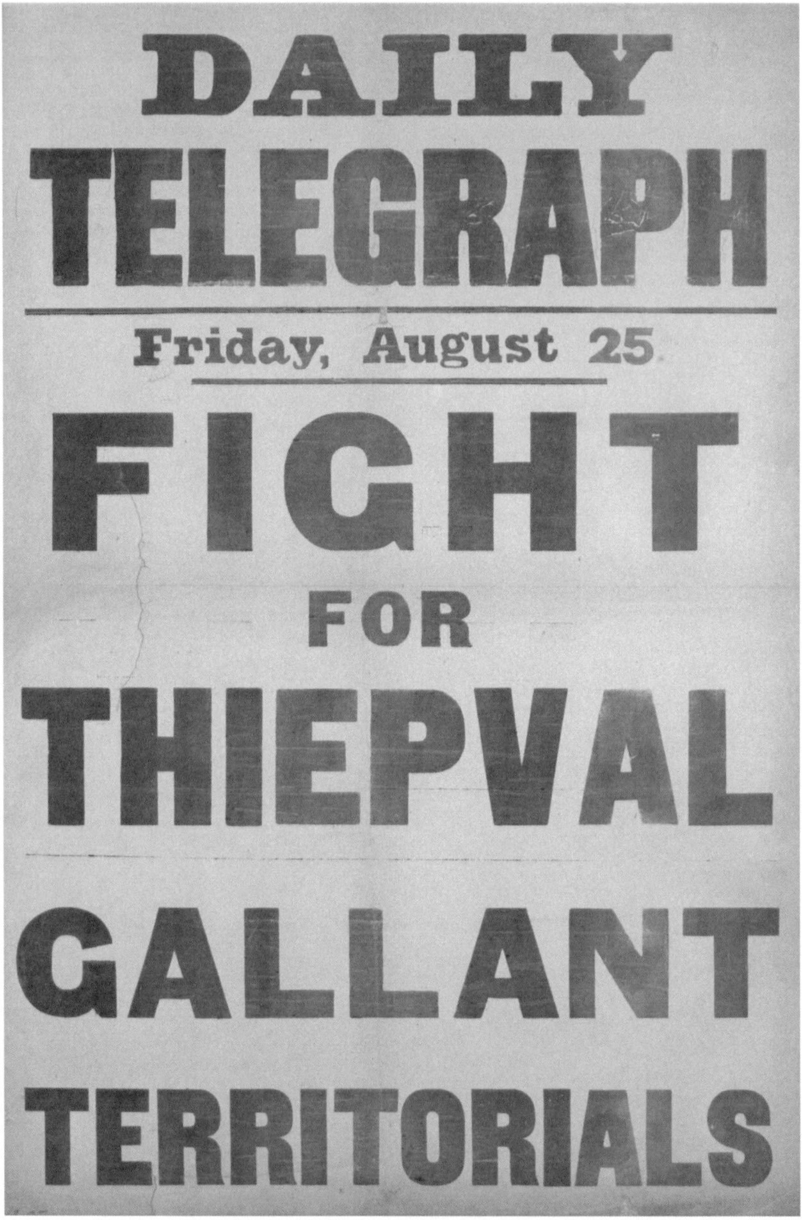

© IWM (Art.IWM PST 12968)

Thiepval Wood

A view across the battle-scarred landscape at Thiepval Wood. There are barely any trees, only several shattered trunks remaining.

William Orpen © IWM (art.IWM ART 2998)

The Death of Edward Iredale

Edward Elisha Iredale was killed in action on 29th August 1916, near Thiepval.

There is a witness report of Edward's death in Lyn MacDonald's book "Somme" which was published in 1985. The witness was Lieutenant Arthur Wilson, of Edward's battalion. They had moved forward to a position right under the German wire where they were subject to such furious shelling that Wilson wondered that any of them had escaped alive. There were enormous casualties. Wilson reported that "Most of the Company commanders were killed - there was no one to lead the men", and sadly Edward was one of them - killed by a blast from a shell which narrowly missed Lieutenant Wilson. He added that we were simply blown to blazes and couldn't do a thing.

Edward is buried in Connaught Cemetery, Thiepval, which is a few hundred yards from the area known as "the Pope's Nose" on the front line, where he fell.

His family subsequently received letters from his Captain, Lieutenant and Chaplain, which are reproduced here.

29th August 1916

Dear Mrs Iredale,

I write with the deepest regret and sympathy to tell you that your son was killed today, a shrapnel bullet striking him on the chest and loss of consciousness following practically at once. This fact at least will have prevented him from suffering any pain.

As you know he was my Company Sgt Major and a splendid fellow in every sense of the word. He displayed at all times the greatest courage and set a fine example to everyone. I twice recommended him for distinction. His death is to me and to all his comrades a very heavy loss.

Again, offering you my deep sympathy in your loss.

I remain

Yours very truly

P Manderville Capt.

O/C A. Company

France 29th August 1916

Dear Mrs Iredale

  Captain Manderville has written to convey to you the sad tidings of our loss but I cannot help adding my own expression of deepest sympathy and sorrow. The death of your son is a great personal loss to me. He was in every way a splendid fellow and the fact that he had attained the rank of Company Sgt Major at his early age speaks for itself.

It may be some small comfort to you to know that he suffered no pain and that he will be buried in the British cemetery near here where his grave will be properly marked and attended to.

Believe me

Yours sincerely

Arthur Gaunt Lieutenant

15th/16th September

Dear Mrs Iredale,

  As Wesleyan chaplain of the brigade to which your son's regiment belongs, I want to add my words of sympathy to the many which you will have received since his death.

Strange as it may seem, I only heard of his death yesterday from his cousin in the same regiment. Times have been so strenuous lately and ordinary arrangements so interrupted that it has been impossible to keep in close touch with all our men and consequently some have been killed and buried and no notification has reached the chaplain concerned.

I was deeply moved yesterday when I heard the sad news, for your son had attended my services both in the open air and at my billet and I had often chatted with him in one place and another. I can assure you that he was a man held in high esteem in the regiment and his loss will be felt.

You will have already have heard how he died and when one remembers the awful suffering one has witnessed, it is a matter for thankfulness that he passed away without pain and especially that he passed away with a prayer upon his lips. God has gathered him to himself and he is safe. May the God of all consolation come near to you in your sorrow and cheer you for, as the men out here often say, yours is the heavier end of the burden.

I am

Yours very sincerely

Fred R Brown

Chaplain

1st W R Field Ambulance

B E F

A Trench, Thiepval

A view of a trench scattered with debris. Splintered wood and sandbags protrude from the large earth trench walls, with a British Army steel helmet and a few boots scattered on the trench floor in the foreground. A few tree stumps stand in the left background and there is a single wooden cross in the distance to the right.

William Orpen © IWM (art.IWM ART 2386)

Yorkshire Herald

TRIBUTES TO TADCASTER PATRIOTS WHO HAVE FALLEN.

Special reference was made at the Tadcaster Wesleyan Chapel, on Sunday, to two local men who have been killed in action.

The first of these was Acting-Sergt.-Major Edward Elisha Iredale, West Yorkshire Regiment, third son of Mr. Charles Iredale, postman, Hodgson's Yard, and of Mrs. Iredale. For going out for a wounded man several months ago, Elisha was recommended for the Distinguished Conduct Medal. On that occasion he was wounded. Deceased met his death on August 29th, being killed by shrapnel He has two brothers serving—one at Salonica and the other with the R.A.M.C. in France. He was employed at the Brewery before the outbreak of war.

The other man alluded to was Private Albert Clayden, K.O.Y.L.I., son of Mr. and Mrs. Clayden, Chapel-street, who died from wounds on August 27th, having been wounded in the arm, back, and right leg. He joined the Army nearly three years ago, and went to the front in October, 1914. He would have been 21 years of age next month. For four months he was at home suffering from "trench" feet. He was formerly employed at the Post Office and at the Brewery. He has two older brothers serving.

Private Clayton, West Yorkshire Regiment, the only son of Mrs. Clayton, St. Joseph-street, has also been killed in action. Before joining the Army he was employed as a tailor.

YORKS. WAR AWARDS.

POSTHUMOUS HONOUR FOR TADCASTER SOLDIER.

Amongst the posthumous honours awarded to non-commissioned officers and men, for bravery in the field, is that of the Military Medal to Lance-Sergeant Edward Elisha Iredale, West Yorkshire Regiment, one of the three soldier sons of Mr. C. Iredale, a well known Tadcaster postman, and of Mrs. Iredale. The deceased was only 19 years of age at the time he met his death, now nearly six months ago. He joined the West Yorkshire Regiment in the first month of the war, was wounded n November, 1915, on the Yser Canal, and was recommended for the Distinguished Conduct Medal. Two days before he was killed he was recommended for a Russian decoration. One brother, William W., is a sapper in the Royal Engineers, and another, Private C. Iredale, is in the R.A.M.C. Both are in Macedonia. The deceased was a clerk at Messrs. John Smith's Brewery before the outbreak of war. His cousin, Private Fred Terry, was killed in France in October last.

12 September 1916 and 24 February 1917

Honours and Awards

Edward Elisha Iredale was awarded the Military Medal for gallantry as he fought in the trenches of Belgium & France. His superiors initially recommended him for the DCM (Distinguished Conduct Medal) but, on review, this was downgraded which was not an unusual occurrence at the time.

The Military Medal was instituted in March 1916, for acts of bravery, by non commissioned officers and men. Edward's award was listed in the London Gazette and the Edinburgh Gazette on 21 February 1917.

He was also recommended for a "Russian Decoration" for his actions but this was never awarded.

Edward's grave says DCM and MM. This is not correct and contemporary images of the grave show this anomaly. The original erroneous specification for the headstone had this error manually corrected, but for some reason that correction was not put into effect.

Commemoration

Edward's name appears on the War Memorial in Westgate, Tadcaster, along with other men of the town who gave up their lives in the Great War. He is also named on the memorials in St Mary's Church and the Methodist Church.
After the war his parents received a named Memorial Plaque, one of over a million that were issued to the next-of-kin of those who had died as a consequence of the war.

The dedication of Tadcaster War Memorial on 30th July 1921

In Flanders Fields

"In Flanders Fields" is in one of the most famous and iconic poems written in the Great War.

It achieved immediate popularity and became synonymous with the sacrifice of those who gave their lives in the First World War and inspired the use of the poppy to commemorate that sacrifice.

It was written by Canadian John McCrae who was moved to write it after the death in action of his friend Alexis Helmer. It was written in early 1915 while he was stationed at Essex Farm which was an Advanced Dressing Station near Ypres. It was the same Essex Farm where Edward was initially treated after sustaining his injury in November 1915, before being repatriated.

Essex Farm is also the site of the Memorial of the 49th West Riding Division, and the final resting place of several West Yorkshire soldiers, including Lieutenant Briggs and Cecil Yates.

In Flanders fields the poppies blow
Between the crosses, row on row,
That mark our place; and in the sky
The larks, still bravely singing, fly
Scarce heard amid the guns below.

We are the Dead. Short days ago
We lived, felt dawn, saw sunset glow,
Loved and were loved, and now we lie
In Flanders fields.

Take up our quarrel with the foe:
To you from failing hands we throw
The torch; be yours to hold it high.
If ye break faith with us who die
We shall not sleep, though poppies grow
In Flanders fields.

Memorials

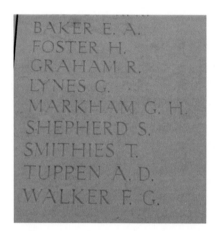 

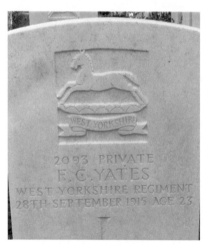 

Memorials to men whose deaths are recorded in the diary

Research Sources

- The Prince of Wales's Own Regiment of Yorkshire, Museum and Archive
- Commonwealth War Graves Commission
- York Explore Library
- York Army Museum
- Staff of 36th (Ulster) Division Memorial,
  The Ulster Memorial Tower, Thiepval, France
- Thiepval Visitor Centre, France
- Musee Somme 1916, Albert, France
- In Flanders Fields Museum, Ieper (Ypres), Belgium
- Talbot House, Poperinge, Belgium
- Imperial War Museum
- War Diary 1/5 Battalion, The West Yorkshire Regiment,
  The National Archive
- The West Yorkshire Regiment in the War 1914-1918,
  Everard Wyrall
- Major & Mrs Holt's Battlefield Guides, Tonie and Valmai Holt
  1 Somme
  2 Ypres Salient and Passchendaele
- Walking the Somme, Paul Reed
- Somme Mud, EPF Lynch ed Will Davies
- Somme, Lyn Macdonald
- www.ww1battlefields.co.uk